BUGS UP CLOSE!

BUTTERFLIES UP CLOSE

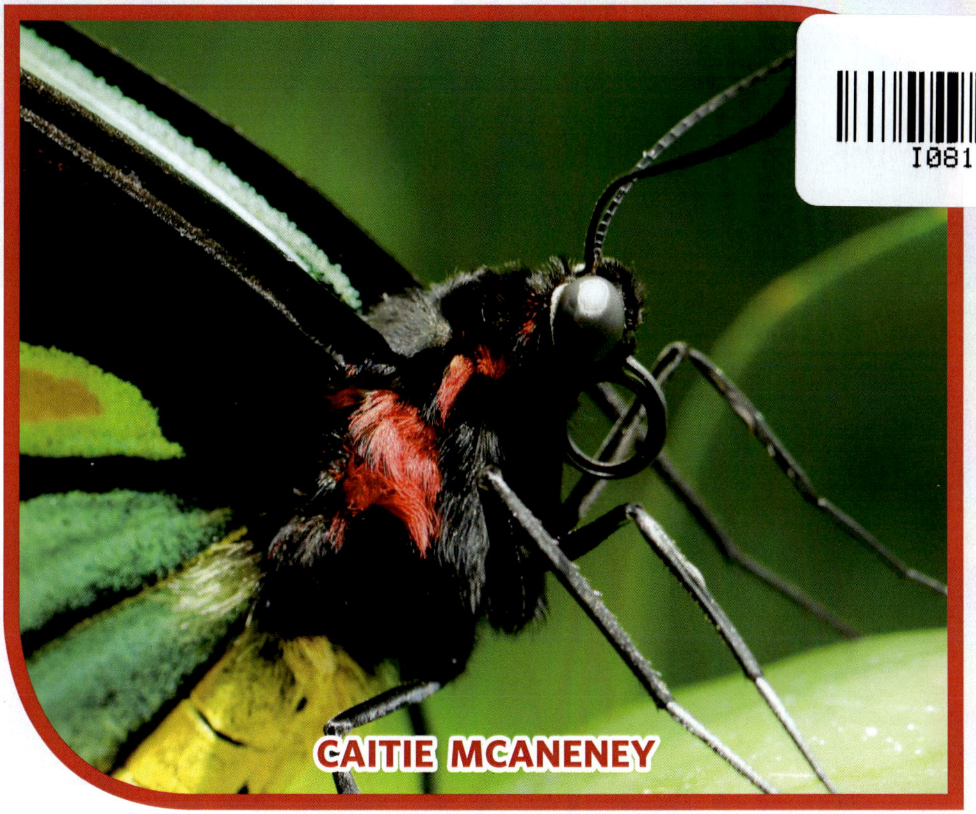

CAITIE MCANENEY

PowerKiDS press.
New York

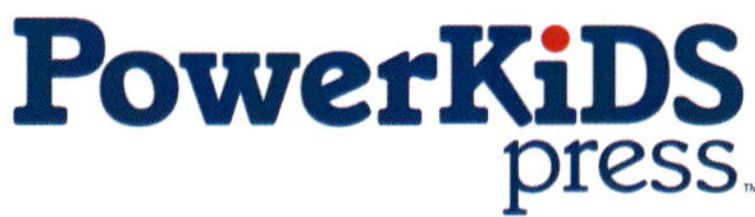

Published in 2020 by The Rosen Publishing Group, Inc.
29 East 21st Street, New York, NY 10010

First Edition

Editor: Elizabeth Krajnik
Book Design: Michael Flynn

Photo Credits: Cover, p. 1 Samantha Hopley/Shutterstock.com; (series background) Karuka/Shutterstock.com; pp. 5, 7 Steven R Smith/Shutterstock.com; p. 6 Breck P. Kent/Shutterstock.com; p. 8 nechaevkon/Shutterstock.com; p. 9 John A. Anderson/Shutterstock.com; p. 11 IrinaK/Shutterstock.com; p. 13 Denis Vesely/Shutterstock.com; p. 15 Super's Desh/Shutterstock.com; p. 17 Darkdiamond67/Shutterstock.com; p. 19 Patrick Foto/Shutterstock.com; p. 21 JHVEPhoto/Shutterstock.com; p. 22 Butterfly Hunter/Shutterstock.com.

Library of Congress Cataloging-in-Publication Data

Names: McAneney, Caitie, author.
Title: Butterflies up close / Caitie McAneney.
Description: New York : PowerKids Press, [2020] | Series: Bugs up close! | Includes bibliographical references and index.
Identifiers: LCCN 2019019247| ISBN 9781725307827 (paperback) | ISBN 9781725307841 (library bound) | ISBN 9781725307834 (6 pack)
Subjects: LCSH: Butterflies–Juvenile literature. | Butterflies–Life cycles–Juvenile literature. | Butterflies–Habitat–Juvenile literature. | Butterflies–Behavior–Juvenile literature.
Classification: LCC QL544.2 .M298 2020 | DDC 595.78/9–dc23
LC record available at https://lccn.loc.gov/2019019247

Manufactured in the United States of America

CPSIA Compliance Information: Batch #CWPK20. For Further Information contact Rosen Publishing, New York, New York at 1-800-237-9932.

CONTENTS

Beautiful Insects

Butterflies are some of the most beautiful **insects** on Earth. They're found everywhere on Earth except Antarctica. Scientists have found and named more than 165,000 species, or kinds, of butterflies. They come in all colors, sizes, and **patterns**.

From Egg to Adult

All butterflies begin life as tiny eggs. When an egg hatches, the wormlike creature that comes out is called a larva. In time, the larva turns into something called a **chrysalis**. Now it's a pupa. When it comes out of the chrysalis shell, it's an adult.

butterfly egg

Parts of a Caterpillar

Butterfly larvae are called caterpillars. They have three parts: a head, a thorax, and an abdomen. Their head has antennae, mouthparts, and six pairs of simple eyes called ocelli. The thorax has three pairs of true legs. The abdomen has a number of false legs.

ocelli
antenna
leg

The Chrysalis

When the caterpillar is done growing, it becomes a pupa. A butterfly pupa may also be called a chrysalis. The chrysalis is the same color as its surroundings so other animals don't eat it. The pupa begins to change from a caterpillar into a butterfly.

Parts of a Butterfly

An adult butterfly's body has the same main parts as the larva. Butterflies have compound eyes, which means their eyes are made up of hundreds of lenses that make one picture in the **brain**. They also have antennae and a straw-like tongue called the proboscis.

antenna
eye
proboscis

The Thorax

A butterfly's middle part is called the thorax. This includes three parts that are **fused** together. Each part has a pair of legs attached to it. The second and third parts each have a pair of wings attached to them. There are two front wings and two back wings.

The Abdomen

The butterfly's end part is called the abdomen. This has 10 parts that are all connected, allowing the abdomen to bend. These parts are made of hard matter called chitin. The butterfly's **digestive** system, heart, **respiratory** system, and **reproductive** parts are in the abdomen.

Standing Out and Blending In

Some butterflies are bright colors. They stand out to people and other animals. Brightly colored butterflies are often toxic, or harmful to eat. Others blend in with their surroundings. This helps keep them safe from animals, too. The orange oakleaf butterfly's wings look like a dead, brown leaf!

Migration

Some butterflies migrate, or move from one area to another at different times of the year. Painted lady butterflies migrate from Mexico to the Mojave Desert in California to lay eggs. Monarch butterflies migrate thousands of miles each year.

All Around You!

Butterflies are all around you! You just need to take the time to see them. Butterflies visit the flowers on your front porch, stop by the plants in your backyard, and flutter around the playground and other places. Take an up-close look at these beautiful insects!

GLOSSARY

brain: An organ in the head that controls movement, thoughts, feelings, and more.

chrysalis: A butterfly pupa that is turning into an adult and has a hard case surrounding it.

digestive: Relating to digestion, or the body's process of changing food into simpler forms that can be taken up and used.

fuse: To become joined as if by melting together.

insect: A small animal that has six legs and a body formed of three parts and that may have wings.

pattern: Repeated forms or shapes.

reproductive: Relating to reproduction, or the act or process of making babies.

respiratory: Relating to respiration, or the act or process of breathing.

INDEX

WEBSITES

Due to the changing nature of Internet links, PowerKids Press has developed an online list of websites related to the subject of this book. This site is updated regularly. Please use this link to access the list: www.powerkidslinks.com/buc/butterflies